Tangible Times

Poems by *Tangela Yvette Cooke*

© 2003 by Tangela Yvette Cooke. All rights reserved.

No part of this book may be reproduced, stored in a retrieval system, or transmitted by any means, electronic, mechanical, photocopying, recording, or otherwise, without written permission from the author.

ISBN: 1-4107-6991-7 (e-book)
ISBN: 1-4107-6990-9 (Paperback)

Library of Congress Control Number: 2003095068

This book is printed on acid free paper.

Printed in the United States of America
Bloomington, IN

Design Cover by
Tangela Y. Cooke
6866 Timber Clair Court
Lithonia, Georgia 30305

1stBooks – rev. 09/25/03

Dedicated to my Father in heaven.
I can do all things through You who strengthens me.

Time cools, time clarifies; no mood can be maintained
quite unaltered through the course of hours.
-Mark Twain

Contents

This Thing Called Love 1

I Am Love 3
Love's Revelations 4
Unlucky in Love 5
I Know… 6
I Love You a Lot 7
The Difference 8
I Never 9
On Making Love 12
Lovesick 14

Relationtrips 15

Visions of You 17
The Cradle Robber and the Grave Digger 18
Don't Waste My Time 19
Te Lee Vizhen 20
Tangie's Prayer 21
Heaven Sent 23
Liar's Game 24
Holy Ghost Marriage 25
TOWGA 26
Spoiled Rotten 27
Your Words Can't Kill My High 28
The Unorthodox Wedding 30
Mr. Right Now 31
The Job-Relationship Connection 32
Letting Go 33
Celibacy 34

It's a Family Affair 35

Glendinia Holmes 37
I Remember Mama - Cinquain and Haiku 38
Daddy Joe - A Sentimental Stream of Consciousness 39
Unqualified Father 42
Sis 45
Nita Blessing (Poetic Need a Blessing) 46
Forget Me Not 48
Onstage Live Revue at the Atrium – Featuring Caj 49
To My Nieces 50

Self-full (It's all About Me) 51

I Am Somebody Special: a personal affirmation 53
Tangela – Made in America 54
My Inspiration 55
The Origin of Cookie 56
15 Years 57
My Testimony 58
I Dwell, So What..59
Patience 60
This Woman of God...61

I Think, Therefore I Write 63

It's a…Poem! 65
Prayer Changes Things 66
It's About Time 67
Steppin' Into Life 68
Soul is……..69
Dark and Lovely...70
Heel to Toe 71
Diamante Poems...72

Stoetry: Poetic storytelling at its best 73

Lucky 75
A Lesson for Prolific Mamas 76
A View to a Kill 77
Fallen Angel..78
Day Dreamin'...80
20/20 81
The House that Love Built 82
The Feet, And Nothing But The Feet, So Help Me God 83
You Left 84
I-95 85

Through My Window 87

The Drought 89
Rain 90
Let It Rain 91
The Hurricane 92
Rainbows...93

Therapoetic Rhyme & Reason 95

The Essence of Adolescence Part I: I heard you 98
The Essence of Adolescence Part II: Are you listening? 100
I Surrender 103
Who Am I? 104
Happiness, A Camouflage 106
Think Before You Speak 107
A Tear For a Purpose 108
To Die For 110
Sticks and Stones 111
Metamorphic 112
Debutante 113
Permission 114
Discouraged 115

To the Kidz, ... 117
From Auntie

Children 119
The Brain 120
Why Homework? 121
The Courageous One 122
The Mind 123

Tangible Times

This Thing Called Love

One word frees us of all the weight and pain of life:
That word is love.
-Sophocles

Tangela Yvette Cooke

I Am Love

I am the flexibility of the heart
Too elastic to be torn apart

I am the most valuable goal to be achieved on earth

More important than money and all its worth

I am something you can give and are compelled to take

I am not counterfeit, phony or fake

I am part of the fundamentals of life
I am why a man has a wife

I am the most serious thing everyone wishes to have

Occasionally forming a tear or sometimes just a laugh

I am security, fondness and feeling
I am disclosed, I am revealing

I bring you joy, fulfillment and pleasure
I am a gift, a surprise, and a treasure

I am what is given from God, in heaven above
I am affection, I am love

Love's Revelations

Love, I once thought, was a beautiful thing.
I thought it was romantic beyond imagination,
like being in a dream world,
reaching the end of the rainbow,
floating on the ocean's floor,
all these things and even more.

It's just hell,
a burning desire,
a restless thing that never tires,
It's what's wanted,
but what's declined once received.
It's a classical situation, hardly ever believed.

Its definition is too intricate to define.
Its reality is too complex to be mine.

Love, I once thought, fulfilled all imagination.
I thought it blossomed into everlasting happiness,
like acquiring pleasures with that pot of gold.
With wishing ceased, dreams unfold,
the ocean conquered, the sky to soar,
all these things and the world galore.

But it's just hell,
a burning desire,
a restless thing that never tires.
It's what's wanted,
but what's declined once received.
It's a classical situation too incredible to believe.

That's love in my eyes, the way it seems.
Sometimes it's a nightmare, other times it's a dream.

Unlucky in Love

I'll take a four-leaf clover and a rabbit's foot
and that charm with the number seven.
Then perhaps I'll get that engagement ring
and when I die, I'll go to heaven.

I committed ten years to one man
and received one empty proposal.
I gave another almost three
and zero was still the total.

My love, loyalty and light-heartedness
proved not to be enough;
and my efforts to achieve the ring
revealed the goings of the tough.

Maybe if I walk down a street one day
I'll see a penny and pick it up...
Then I'll win the lottery
because in the love game, I have no luck.

Tangela Yvette Cooke

I Know...

How do I know...
Because it feels so intoxicating and so
exciting to be with you and be
with you even when you're not around.
I feel so uninhibited to look, to feel, to touch, to taste
and to not just listen, but to hear every word you say.
The light inside me is shining, glimmering, and projecting brightly.
Can you see it?
It's reflected in my voice, and my smile
and it's radiantly beaming through the windows of my soul.
My mind is clear.
My thinking is coherent.
How I feel does not have to be debated, rationalized or argued
because I know it's real, faithfully.
I feel empowered, motivated and spiritually connected
to God, you and my life all at the same time.
I'm overwhelmed in a good way.
I'm truly exhilarated.
I've longed for this feeling all of my life.
I know...*I love you* and this feeling is real and right on time.

I Love You a Lot

"How much do you love me?"
you query.
Enough to make the strongest mind
grow weary.

How can I quantify
the love I feel for you?
What superlative will be enough
or make THIS MUCH a cue?

How do I love thee, now let *me* count the ways
No, I'll leave that up to
Elizabeth Barret Browning
because I could go on for days.

Gordon, I love you. I love you. I love you.
What more can I do or say?
Gordon, I love you. I love you. I love you,
and from my heart's mouth I convey.

"How much do you love me?"
you ask.
…enough to not make measuring,
how much, a task.

My love for you has no degrees, powers,
or exponential notations;
because infinity is as measurable as
my mind's rotations.

My thoughts sometimes circle.
They spin round and round.
They go back and forth
to this love that I've found.

Yet I can't count the number of times
and the "I love yous" that I think and feel.
Just know that the quantity is a lot.
Moreover, the quality is real.

Gordon, I love you. I love you. I love you.
No petal says "loves me not."
Gordon, I love you. I love you. I love you
and the how much is a lot.

Tangela Yvette Cooke

The Difference

To LOVE someone and to be IN LOVE with someone are not the same.

LOVE is a prerequisite to being IN LOVE.

However, you don't have to be IN LOVE to LOVE.

The "IN" part is what gives the two diverse meanings.

The "IN" part is what makes the two totally different emotions.

To be IN LOVE is to be INto someone emotionally, spiritually and psychologically.

As a matter of fact, being IN LOVE can be likened to feeling INtoxicated.

To be IN LOVE is to take the relationship to a higher level, the physical realm.

Thus, to be IN LOVE involves INtimacy.

To be IN LOVE is to be actively INvolved in his life.

To be IN LOVE is to be INspired to please him and seduce him.

Being IN LOVE comes from the INside.

It's an INner feeling that helps you accept, overlook and/or tolerate his flaws and idiosyncrasies.

Being IN LOVE is to be free of all of your INhibitions while you're with him.

To be IN LOVE takes some degree of INtelligence because it is serious, not a game.

And it's definitely not the same as being INfatuated.

Not only is being IN LOVE fun, exciting and INteresting.

Being IN LOVE is also INcomparable to being IN anything else.

Tangible Times

I Never

I never surmised
that to gaze
into
your greenish-gray
eyes
that I would
become weak.
from your vibe,
your voice,
the words you speak.
I'm captivated,
enthralled
and hypnotized.
Snap your fingers,
Eros.
because I'm
mesmerized.

I never conceived
that I'd
easily believe
every word
that you speak.
I'm half naked
in five minutes
from my head
to my feet.
You I can trust,
your voice,
seductive
and soothing
it makes
me relaxed
and prepared
for your wooing.

I never voiced
that you make me
moist
with just the
touch of
your hand
that feels so
erotic

to the point
that my lips,
my breasts,
my inner thighs
and my entirety
cries for you.

I never felt
that once
you removed
your belt
and shed your
pants
that I'd become
ravished,
enraptured,
and entranced
in your
bed of ecstasy
that penetrates
my mind,
body and
soul.

I would never
conclude
that I would
exude
joy
from reciprocated
passion,
the ultimate intimacy,
not sex,
but the
physical and
emotional
components
that are used to
create
the art of making love
and its finishing touches.

I never guessed
that when you undressed
ever so slowly
I would succumb

Tangible Times

to the pleasures
of the flesh
and lose myself
in time and
space
because I'm so
into you
and you feel
so good inside of me.

I never knew
that to be with you
intimately
would help me define,
conceptualize and
understand
what it means and
how it feels
to make love.

I never thought
that I would be
caught
surmising,
conceiving,
voicing,
feeling,
concluding and
guessing
that when it comes to intimacy
you have Savoir Faire
and before
you
I only knew
sex,
coitus
and intercourse.

Tangela Yvette Cooke

On Making Love

How does it feel when I massage your feet,
your back and your hand ever so gently?
Does the friction of my hands or fingertips
penetrate your entire body?
Are you able to release and let go of stress?
For me, making love to you is just as soothing.

Do you like the taste of chocolate?
Does it satisfy your taste buds?
Do you take your time eating it
in an effort to savor its flavor
or do you consume it quickly because
you know it might not be there tomorrow?
For me, making love to you is just as delicious.

Have you ever gone on a nature walk?
Have you experienced the peace, serenity or
tranquility from the connection between self, God
and His beautiful earth?
For me making love to you is just as spiritual.

When you hear your favorite song,
do you sometimes feel a chill or thrill
after the singer has hit a certain note
which means he or she can not only sing,
but also can sang?
Did you know the song was a hit,
because you literally felt it?
For me, making love to you feels just as orgasmic.

What does riding a roller coaster feel like?
Do you get a rush when the ride is
descending from its peak at 100 miles per hour?
For me, making love to you feels just as exciting.

Have you ever taken a long hot shower,
dried off and then lain on satin, silk or cotton sheets
dressed like Adam before Eve bit the forbidden fruit?
Have you ever done so while the temperature
was just right and your favorite love songs
were playing on the radio?
Did you like the ambiance
and the way the sheets felt against your skin?
For me, making love to you feels just as sensuous.

Making love to you is like eating chocolate
while bathing under a waterfall and
listening to natures melodies amongst
beautiful mountains and trees
in Eve's attire before the forbidden fruit.
It feels relaxing, delicious, spiritual,
orgasmic, exciting and sensual.
Making love to you feels real good.

Lovesick

I long for you,
especially late at night.
I can't sleep.
Where shall I lie my head?
I'm too good for my pillow
and the mattress just isn't doing the trick.
Your strong chest would be perfect
and your heartbeat plays my favorite lullaby.
I wish you could touch me right now.
I want to be held.
I want to be hugged,
but my teddy bear doesn't hold or hug back.
I yearn for your presence.
I desire to be with you.
Keeping busy gets me through the day
and talking with you on the phone
gets me through the evening,
but the nights are the worse.
Jesus is always here
but you're not
and He made me to compliment
and supplement you.
Although you're only 15 minutes away
and we see each other as often as we can.
I miss you.
Each day I become increasingly nostalgic
for your love.
Sometimes insomnia sets in
because I'm anxious to talk to you,
see you, hear you, feel you
or just be with you.
My heart cries out for you.
I'm lovesick.

Relationtrips

To understand how any society functions you must understand the relationship between the men and the women.
-Angela Davis

Tangela Yvette Cooke

Visions of You

(for Mike S. Litwhiler)

tossing and turning
clear visions of you
married life-
you loving it too

exploring the grounds
of U.M.'s campus
freshmen to seniors
our first love canvas

fulfilling a fantasy
atop a building
the beach, a mountain
never yielding

sequential events
alive in my mind
segueing prayer
unconfined

occurring in REM
and in my bed
disturbing, yet pleasing
all in my head

Tangela Yvette Cooke

The Cradle Robber and the Grave Digger

She's a quarter of century.
He's a little over half.
She's still wet behind the ears.
He's got dirt around one calf.

She dolls up to look like Barbie,
He a conservative toy store clerk.
She's filled with innocence and expectations.
He feels she's just a perk.

She looks forward to love and marriage,
He a companion and toy.
She respects his position in society,
He - his kids bring him joy.

She's showcased like a trophy.
He holds her arm with pride.
She wonders if he takes her seriously,
He the truth he'll hide.

She is blind to age lines and wrinkles.
He likes tight, yet supple skin.
She trades sex for affection and commitment.
He wants to settle down in sin.

She cries in her bed at night,
While he rests in peace.
She wants love, not a father figure,
He a dainty girl in fleece.

Don't Waste My Time

Let's skip the small talk
and get right down to it.
Give me your family, medical,
and sexual history.
For now, that should do it.

My experiences have taught me
that nothing is guaranteed.
You can date him exclusively
for ten years
and it still may not succeed.

So tell me what's up right now.
Put everything on the table
(your interest, values, dreams and goals),
and marriage…
are you ready, willing and able?

A moment with me is valuable
so authenticity, I must exact.
Because I'm giving you a minute
of my time
and I know I'll never get it back.

Tangela Yvette Cooke

Te Lee Vizhen

I have a stay-at-home boyfriend
and he was made just for me.
He keeps me informed and entertained
and stress and worry-free.

No matter how I look or what I wear
my gentle touch turns him on.
I know how to push just the right button
and he's turned off when I'm gone.

Sometimes our nights are filled with drama
and I have to call my sis.
Sometimes he has me so captivated…
household duties, I'm remiss.

He doesn't demand much from me
just my attention and admiration.
Every now and then he'll make a small request
like "tune in to your homeboy's station."

He makes me sing, laugh and cry,
yet I'm always in control
and don't concern myself with infidelity
or my love-life taking its toll.

Now if he can't keep me satisfied
I'll check out his good friend, Boc.
Because this girl likes other stimulation
and she knows just where to look.

Tangie's Prayer

Dear God,

I pray that you'll send
a worthy soul mate
who can comprehend
my philosophy
for a love everlasting.
A monogamous relationship
is my reason for fasting
from a one-night-stand or
a hedonistic life-style.
I want the courtship
that lasts a while,
one that's based on respect,
honesty and faithfulness
an abundance of humor,
passionate love and
playfulness.

He must have goals
to fulfill and pursue.
He must have a job,
because it takes two.

Our dreams and values
should be of one accord.
He must put God first,
my savior and Lord.

I know he'll physically
attract me at first,
but his intelligence and
personality must quench
my thirst
for the second date and
the third and the fourth
through the Nth
then perhaps our wedding date
on October tenth.

Yes, I want him to know
the details of my life
and about my plan
to be his wife.

Tangela Yvette Cooke

I desire to know, honor
and love him
till death do us part and
our minds, bodies and spirits
should mesh from the start.

Communication and
a good friendship
will keep us together…and
a divine commitment
will make *us* forever.

I ask for all these
blessings in Jesus' name
and by this prayer
I stake out my claim.

        Amen

Heaven Sent

You don't know this
but I asked for you before we met.

You were in my prayers.

I said,
"Dear Lord, please send me a man,
not just any man.

Father-God,
Please make him a heterosexual who
is humorous, interesting, intelligent,
goal-oriented, disciplined, youthful,
vibrant, mature, affectionate, loyal,
honest, strong, romantic, attractive,
tall, sexy, passionate, lovable, sensitive,
adventurous, healthy and employed.

Father,
please also make him a non-smoker
who is alcohol, drug, and disease-free
and available to me, for me.

I want to feel what's it is like to love
a complete man, not a boy
or perpetual adolescent.

I want to fall for a Man."

…and then I met you.

THANK GOD!

Tangela Yvette Cooke

Liar's Game

He won his game,
that game that liars play,
to love more than one woman
and never say…

a word or three
is all it took
to end their story,
to close their book…

a twelve year epic
of love and pain
and joy and happiness
despite the rain…

or storm between them
that arose from a path
of indiscretions
that triggered her wrath…

of destruction
from deep anger and hurt,
she packed her bags,
but did she desert…

him, her past
their history
of growth, understanding
and loyalty…?

yes, he won the game
that liars play,
tired of his mistress,
long gone, his fiancée.

Cheaters never win,
though he believes he's won.
Yet he's drinking and dwelling…
and a good woman, he has none.

Holy Ghost Marriage

Our courtship
begin when I was 22.
Rocky times ensued thereafter.
Our unsteady relationship
was a pendulum of love and disbelief
until I submitted and had faith.
We wed eight years later.
He's perfect and He completes me.
You can say that
I see me in Him.
I promise to love, honor and respect Him,
forsaking all others
even after death.
He's everything that I want
Him to be.
He fulfills my needs and
embodies me with love.
I'll do my best
to do right by Him
and I vow to never stop
calling His name.

Tangela Yvette Cooke

TOWGA

Sure there are plenty of fish in the sea:
great ones,
small ones,
clever ones,
quaint ones,
pretty ones,
ugly ones,
delicious ones,
poisonous ones,
and the list goes on in that big, beautiful body of life.
But which one is worth keeping once she's hooked
and how do you know if or when to let her go?
I believe I reeled in "The Catch of the Day"
the other day.
She was a combination of dinner and a trophy.
So I didn't know if I wanted to take her home
or put her on display.
While making my plans for her life
and basking in the glory of my achievement,
She either slipped away or I threw her back.
I can't remember exactly what happened.
My pride tells me it was the latter.
Now this fisherman has an empty plate,
nothing to show and a boat load of regrets.
To me, she'll always be the one who got away
and I know I'll never bait another one like her.

Spoiled Rotten

The last one spoiled me
with rent-free room and board.
Fed me fast food to five stars-
Taxied me in his car-

Treated me to mini vacations
and fun amusement parks-
Paid for the matinees
and movies after dark-

My role was to love him,
respect him and treat him right-
His focus on my money
was out of mind and out of sight-

So if I have to charge it,
sign my check
or go Dutch,
it won't take much

to decline an invitation,
ignore a call or say no-
to checking out a Hawks game
or an Off Broadway show.

Because if I have to spend
you may as well call me Rover
and let me roam and be alone
'cause the relationship is over.

Tangela Yvette Cooke

Your Words Can't Kill My High

You say your boyfriend romanced you
but than the wooing stopped.
He showered you with compliments
but the frequency dropped
and your love-life flopped

because after he got you
his eyes started to wander,
his mind began to ponder
and his heart just grew less fonder.

I really don't care about
what your man does.
I won't apply your experiences
to Jack, just because
and no, I won't let you
ruin my love buzz.

You say Jack is no different
from any other,
a dog chasing cat is like the
typical brother,
so my Mr. Right is just Mr. Another,

because he deceived you
and his feelings were not true
you say give Jack some time
and his real colors will shine through.

I refuse to let you kill my high
although I won't deny
that I will be disheartened
if Jack's love is a lie.

You say that we'll never marry
because we're two of the same
and his life-style will bore me
and a breakup will claim
the fun and the passion,
so I won't take his name,

because you think I was meant
for a man in my past
who is of the same race, age and caste
and since our personalities clash
you think that he and I might last.

I won't let my sister's illogic and negativity
or my friends generalizations and mediocrity
bring me down
or get the best of me.

You can say whatever you want
the locksmith for my heart
only God can appoint
our relationship, I know He will anoint,

because head bowed,
while on my knees
I know my Father has heard my pleas
and now I have my wings,
and Jack has his keys.

I want to fly away
I want to live day by day
and intoxicated with Jack
I'll stay.

Tangela Yvette Cooke

The Unorthodox Wedding

You married me when you slept with me.
Intercourse, love-making, coitus, or sex
was our nuptial.
Love, honor and respect
obviously brought us to this point.
We did not enter a church or courtroom
because your bedroom
was much more convenient.
And your bed was a lot less
intimidating than an alter.
Passion gave me away
and we tacitly said our vows,
because our lips were locked
and our tongues were tied up.
Slipping myself onto you
and you into me
was symbolic of the ring ceremony.
We said "I do" when we "did it".
the preacher or judge and witnesses
were God and your four walls.
Our orgasms at the end of our consensual union
conveyed the excitement and celebration
of our life-long commitment,
the most sacred and holiest of matrimonies.

Mr. Right Now

Yes, my dear, you are the one,
that I have chosen for me.
You are the man, everyday,
I would like to see.

I'm past puppy love and beyond infatuation,
I know you are the one I need.
A splendid feeling, in any case,
you are right for me, indeed.

You've made me feel wanted, so I'm not disappointed,
because I've gotten what I prayed for.
You're handsome, humorous, intelligent, polite
and certainly not a bore.

If it's love for two weeks, a month,
or even more than a year.
I'm glad to share it with someone
of whom I think sincere.

My last words are to convey my thoughts
of what I think of you.
you are a beautiful person inside and out
and this compliment beams through.

The Job-Relationship Connection

Am I looking for
casual or termination at will
or noncommittal, like a dead-end job
or do I want it to lead to marriage or a contract
(that guarantees ownership interest)?

Am I ready for interviews or first meetings
with questions like would your last place of employment rehire you
or would your ex take you back
and why were you fired or why did you leave?

Getting hired or falling in love
leads to a probation or a courtship to get to know you better
and an observation of your skills and talents
to determine what more do you have to bring
and have brought to the table
and the quality of your work.

Considering the fact that people quit and partnerships dissolve,
will it work or will a conflict of interest or infidelity ever be an issue
and will you ever feel the need to moonlight or cheat?

Do your co-workers or new family like, respect, or even accept your work
or when you work, does your work speak for itself?

Because reality dictates that a successful career
or relationship requires hard work and commitment.

The practice of good work ethic or honesty
combined with a sense of job fulfillment or love
advances to a decision to retain you or an engagement,
a natural progression,
(a promotion or wedding segueing)
with promises of raises or prosperity
and many other benefits.

Marriage is a job.

Letting Go

To the men I've loved, liked and lusted for before

Hello,
You've reached the present.
Sorry you've missed me.
If this is Mike,
please take a hike.
If this is Jeff,
I'm glad you left.
If this is Jack,
I don't want you back.
And for the rest,
it was for the best.
Because if you want
a love that lasts.
Don't look for a future
in the past.
But thank you for calling.

Tangela Yvette Cooke

Celibacy

Kiss me,
hug me, and
love me,
not sexually,
but sensually
and intercourse-free.

Respect me,
appreciate me, and
celebrate me
by committing to be
sex–free.

Connect to me
touch me intimately
while abstaining
with me
and sharing intimacy
in a state of celibacy.

It's a Family Affair

Only a life lived for others is a life worthwhile.
-Albert Einstein

Tangela Yvette Cooke

Glendinia Holmes

(February 14, 1945 – May 27, 1979)

Born on Valentine's Day,
Dina's love was here to stay.

As a proud, single parent of five lovely kids,
she raised us right. That's what she did!

The most wonderful mother of them all
nurtured, taught and fed us. She was on the ball.

With a radiant personality and an incandescent smile,
Mom's strong character gave meaning to style.

She treated us with love, kindness and understanding
without being to critical, fussy or demanding.

She made us happy and kept us together.
Within us, her love lasts always and forever.

Through timeless love and memories that transcend…
our mother remains with us until the end.

And in our hearts we'll always know
that Glendinia's love will never go.

Tangela Yvette Cooke

I Remember Mama

Cinquain

Forget?
Never, I love
her too much. I'll cherish
moms memories forever. Your
daughter

Haiku

Beautiful I saw
a woman as lovely as
my mom, Glendinia

Daddy Joe
A Sentimental Stream of Consciousness
(February 17, 1932 – February 21, 1988)

Butterfly, butterfly
fly to my father
whisper that I love him.

I loved being a child
until I turn fourteen.
I loved myself, my life, my family,
and especially my daddy.
And don't you say anything
bad about my daddy.

When I reminisce
about my real father,
my daddy,
the man I placed on a pedestal before mama died,
I smile inside.
He was charming, tall, dark and handsome.

On weekends daddy would pick us up,
and take us to his hang-out, under The Tree.
While we played and ate cookies,
candy, pickles, hot sausages,
potato chips and other junk foods,
he and his friends got their drink on.

At daddy's apartment
he played games with us
like Monopoly, Spades and 21.
He especially liked playing cards.
He also taught us how to deal and shuffle.
He had a comfy bachelor pad
with a phone inside a box and other knickknacks.

He had been a veteran, an airplane mechanic,
an auto mechanic, a professional bus driver,
a security guard and a bus mechanic.
He received a Purple Heart from
the Army after one of those wars.
He was both academic and street smart,
although he had to drop out of high
school to support his mom and siblings.

Tangela Yvette Cooke

He loved to buy old cars.
I remember the gray car that shimmied
when he drove me to Edison Middle,
the brown station wagon that I convinced him
to let me park when he knew I couldn't even drive,
the white pick-up truck with the camper on back
that looked like a turtle,
the yellow car that he said I would own
as soon as I graduated from high school
and the orange car that never left the driveway.

And cook, he was the best,
Most of his soul food recipes called for
six onions, three green peppers
and eight cloves of garlic.
He'd say, "This is how they cook in the Bahamas."
They tell me he taught my mama how to cook.

"Tangie, little Tangie, three pennies I pray,"
he'd sing to me in his smooth,
Sam Cooke-like voice.

Sometimes when I cried
after someone had hurt my feelings
he'd treat me like a baby
and say, "Do you want daddy to shoot 'em."
Man did I feel safe as long as daddy was alive.
Other times he'd just tickle me
until I forgot about my tears.

I recall running to him and jumping in his arms
on Fridays after coming home for school.
"Daddy!, Daddy!," I'd yell in excitement.
He'd smile and greet me with a kiss.

Most of his friends respected and/or feared him.
He refrained from cursing in front of us.
He admonished his friends to do the same.
Once he tried to teach my younger brother,
Junior, how to shoot a shotgun,
and he almost shot a man,
who also hung around under The Tree.
Instead of the target [the man] getting angry,
he thanked my dad for saving his life.
Joe Cooke was BAD,
and everyone under The Tree knew it.

I used to think he was immortal.
Dad was shot 15 times
and he was also stabbed by a gang of teenagers,
but he survived.
An aneurysm took him out,
a ruptured cerebral aneurysm.

This forty-something year old man
was the epitome of the perpetual adolescent,
a lovable big brother of sorts.
He told jokes and always made us laugh.
He was just fun to be around.
He was always broke,
at least that's what he told us.
But it didn't matter to me because
it was cool hangin' with my daddy.

He was a lady's man.
I met at least four of his girlfriends:
Hattie Mae,
Peaches,
Erline,
Evelyn,
and I'm sure there were many and more than that.
He always said that I had 18 other brothers and sisters
that I did not know about.

People would tell us that "Joe" was a big liar.
They would say bad things about him.
Not my daddy,
I wasn't hearing them [until I turned 14].
In my eyes, dad was the greatest.
He was certainly my hero.

He always told us that he loved us.
He'd say, "I'll die for my children."
No wonder I felt safe.

Those were the good old days.
How I miss my fun-loving, weekend daddy.
Unfortunately,
daddy stayed and left me
before he physically died.
I guess full-time parenting can kill a man's spirit.

How I miss my daddy.

Tangela Yvette Cooke

Unqualified Father

The position was empty,
yet no one applied:
A full-time custodian needed
to stand by their side.

The mother had died
and a guardian was wanted.
There was a man
biologically appointed.

He was alleged to be a drunk,
a liar, and a sinner,
the lowest or the low or
furthest from a winner.

He saw the ad
and thought it was It.
All the duties were there,
the job hard to quit.

He could lose opportunities,
such as running the streets.
His many woman friends
would be hard to treat.

He would have to sacrifice
and work hard to earn a living.
Children, clothes, food, rent –
all his money made for giving.

He took custody of his children
and the first year went great
he even helped them with their homework
and recruited a mate.

She was very generous
and did what she could.
So he charmed her and used her
like a true player would.

He would spend her money,
while he toyed with her heart.
He was a great pretender,
and he knew his part.

Tangible Times

She took care of the children,
and treated them well.
But what she didn't know
is that she was living a tale.

Many of the qualifications
that he thought he had
were left undiscovered
his work was bad.

And the position, "Father,"
that he'd applied for
he found out one year later,
for him, was a bore.

So he decided to run the streets,
drink, smoke and have fun.
He chose to neglect
his daughters and son.

He chose to live *his* life to the fullest
because fatherhood wasn't his calling.
Even the so-called deadbeat dads
found his behavior appalling.

So strong devotion from his family
was a benefit that he lost
and his children's unconditional love
was another considerable cost.

He'd ignored his position
as a father or dad
and all the duties
that he had:

Such as nurturing, nourishing,
and spending quality time,
teaching, showing interest…,
and cultivating young minds.

But since he had a binding contract
he didn't brood about being fired.
And since no one else desired the job
a replacement was never hired.

Tangela Yvette Cooke

> The person to whom this position belongs,
> I really shouldn't bother,
> but it's Joseph Simeon Cooke, Sr.,
> alias, the Unqualified Father.

Sis

I thank God for creating sisters to love,
a sort of guardian angel sent from above.

To make life easier and to temper bad feelings,
a sister can help and is able and willing.

I have a special sister, with whom I get along,
one who gives me examples of what's right and what's wrong.

When our mom died and I felt all alone,
sis stepped right in and made her house my home.

For almost two years she cared for lil' bro and me.
She was only seventeen and as altruistic as can be.

This sister is kind, considerate and sharing
of thoughts, television or clothes for wearing.

She's the kind of sister, if she makes you mad,
you can forgive and forget anything bad.

She's black, beautiful and quite a lady.
She's intelligent, strong and sometimes crazy.

She's the next best thing to having a mother.
A quintessential friend compared to all the others.

She's independent, honest and knows about life:
jobs, opportunities and being a wife.

I love this young lady with all my heart
and with help from God we will never part.

We can disagree, joke and just kid around, but she'll always get my respect.
She has earned it, thus deserves it, so this I won't neglect.

I praise her for the person she is and she remains on the top of my list.
Linda Antoinette Jackson [Small] is a very special big sis.

Tangela Yvette Cooke

Nita Blessing

(Poetic Need a Blessing)

Our wonder years had a rough beginning
and taunts from you were never-ending.

I used to believe you hated me.
"Baldy, skinny, awky, bony."
Why? Now you see.

Remember when you punched me *in* my stomach?
It wasn't enough that you called me names.
When baby-sitting became your problem
your little sister was to blame.

Your behavior in the past was probably the norm
through sociological eyes.
Because your love for me became overwhelming
and the hatefulness ceased and died.

God truly works in mysterious ways
and our relationship is just one case
of how hidden blessings are revealed to us
at the right time and in the right place.

What a wonderful big sister you turned out to be,
my ace-boon coon and protector of me.

You have dads boldness and moms generous heart –
revealed at our rivalry's end and our camaraderie's start.

You missed my high school graduation,
but you made sure that you were there for college
and for this I am grateful
and must take time to acknowledge.

I thank you for McDonalds, the Omni
and Morningside Park.
You brightened many of my days
though my teen years seemed dark.

I thank you for my nieces and nephew
who are very special in my life.
I thank you for the retreat to you place
from dad's neglect and my strife.

Tangible Times

Now, as and adult I know that you love me
from your words and acts as a friend.
With all the care and concern that you show me,
it seems your heart's depth has no end.

Yes, God does work in mysterious ways
and I can say this without guessing
because despite our distant childhood history
to Tangela, Nita is a blessing.

Tangela Yvette Cooke

Forget Me Not

(for my brother Joe)

Though the days are rapidly passing,
and in time we will depart,
there is one thing that I ask of you:
keep me in your heart.

As our lives go on and on,
each going different ways,
remember the times we shared together
during my high school and college days.

When you reach success on top,
looking down on the others,
there is one thing I hope you do:
sing our memories, my brother.

If you're ever lonely, sick or tired of living
and praying for an end,
there is one thing I'd beg of you,
forget me not, I'm your friend.

Onstage Live Revue at the Atrium – Featuring Caj

(observations from The Atrium in Stone Mountain, GA on 12/19/02)

He was Put'n It Down
and praisin' them
He was croonin' the chorus
and amazin' them
God, family, his fiancée
and best friend too,
"Where would I be,
be without you…"
All hands were waving
from side to side.
All body parts were in motion
as each soul felt the vibe.
Oh how his presence
did manifest,
showcasing his talent,
his gift no less.
Where would he be,
if not livin' his dream…?,
Offstage and not livin'.
Bump that, Caj sing.

Tangela Yvette Cooke

To My Nieces

For Keisha, Mesha, Toiya, Isha and Tiffany

Take time to know Tom, Dick or Harry
before you let him in your house.
Better yet, get to know his history
before he becomes your spouse.

The difference between the walls I live in
and the walls that reside in me
is I don't have to dwell within my walls
but the ones in me aren't free.

Decisions you make can affect your life
some choices are not simple.
Just remember to put yourself first
because your body *is* a temple.

It can take a year to know Tom or Harry
and Dick, more than a while.
Know that there's no need to rush
and like my daddy said, "Dick won't go out of style."

If your walls could talk, I'd hope they'd say
our keeper is very clever.
And I'd hope you would be able to discern
what's love and what's forever.

Self-full
(It's all About Me)

The most difficult thing in life is to know yourself.
-Thales

Tangela Yvette Cooke

I Am Somebody Special:
a personal affirmation

I am somebody special.
      of mind
I am intelligent.
I am logical.
I am perceptive.
I am somebody special.
      of body
I am slim.
I am toned.
I am strong.
I am somebody special
      of soul
I am spiritual.
I am love.
I am divine.
I am somebody special.
      of aesthetics
I am dark brown.
I am beautiful.
I am exotic.
I am somebody special.
      of the earth
I am unique.
I am a gem.
I am Tangela Yvette Cooke.
I am somebody special.

Tangela – Made in America

Pronounced forehead and slanted eyes
Soft, full lips
Genetic thighs
Long, shapely legs and ugly toes
Nice, small waistline
And a Bahamian nose
Small, bright teeth
Rotund buttocks
Thin, nappy hair twisted into locs
Toasted almond skin
And statuesque frame
A ballerina's collarbone is one in the same
High cheekbones on a round face
Neck like a giraffe – with its length and grace
A hybrid of runner and dancer for sure
She's Africa meets Asia
Yet a North American allure

My Inspiration

Move me.
Amuse me.
Let my muse be
a dip, two lips or a sip
of
depression inspired poetry,
love inspired poetry,
life inspired poetry,
or self inspired poetry.

Move me.
Let my moods be
expressed creatively
through poetry
as a dip, two lips or a sip
for your eyes
to see.

Tangela Yvette Cooke

The Origin of Cookie

Corey called me Cookie in the second grade.
At first I thought he was just a dummy
because he couldn't pronounce
C-O-O-K-E, correctly.

Later I found out
that he had a crush on me,
which caused me to see him in a different light -
one with a twinkle in it.
All of a sudden my new nickname sounded kind of cute.
So I sort of adopted it after that.

It turns out that all of the Cookes
in my immediate family
were called Cookie by their peers too
at one point in their lives (as a nickname
or because the person addressing them
did not know that the E was silent).

I've always been Tangie at home,
Auntie to my nieces and nephews,
Tangela at school or work,
and T, Tan or Tange to the lazy people.
But ever since the dummy,
I've been Cookie everywhere else.

Cookie, yeah that's me.

15 Years

It took 15 years to search and find me
and to love myself unconditionally.

It took 15 years to appreciate life
and to overcome my depression and to end my strife.

It took 15 years to reflect on my past
and to accept my poor choices and let go at last.

It took 15 years to acknowledge every person I've met
and know that there were reasons why our souls did connect.

It took 15 years to know that I am a blessing
and to realize that my experiences taught me valuable lessons.

It took 15 years to look in the mirror and see
God's perfect image or reflection of me.

Tangela Yvette Cooke

My Testimony

Mama died when I was only a dime
and daddy, I'd just turned nineteen,
so during my adolescent years
suicidiation was my theme.

My lonely heart and idle mind
was a playground for the devil,
until I turned twenty-two
and God took me to another level.

He showed me my resiliency
and answered each and every prayer-
law school, grad school, Lackland Air Force Base-
yes, the Lord was there.

Time and time again, I quit,
took detours from my journey
questioning my purpose in life
without allowing Him to turn me.

Surrendering [to Him], but not giving up
has brought peace unto my heart.
He took away my plaguing depression
and gave me a fresh new start.

I Dwell, So What

Please don't give me a hard time,
because in my past, I dwell.
Current events and déjà vu
take me back to hell.

I had to process five long years
of my dad's neglect of me –
how he didn't care if I ate or not
a deadbeat's mentality.

I had to get over feeling inferior
due to a substandard education.
I had to get over not feeling loved
and my early emancipation.

Letting go of memories is hard
and so, in my past I dwell.
Though one forgives, she can't forget.
So, my story, I must tell.

Tangela Yvette Cooke

Patience

Pardon me for paying too close attention,
  but I'm told "good things come to those who wait."
  With my clock ticking and the meter running, it will soon be too late.

After the college years I thought tables might turn.
  I believed a bachelor's degree would be my ticket to earn.

Time is the big problem, and living is what it's about.
  I've had no major breaks or great achievements.
  My span just might run out.

I've been searching for success and I am still young to some.
  Nothing has happened to brag about, and at thirty, life's begun.

Easy life is what I want with a fine job to assure it,
  a promising career, with great outlooks, and a contract to secure it.

Notice how I can't wait to make it and to end my self-perceived strife.
  It would be the greatest sin not to experience God's purpose or the destiny for my life.

Candidly speaking, I want to be rich, I want the finer things, the nice…
  A small apartment, low income – these things just won't suffice.

Eager beaver, yeah that's me, with peace, love, happiness and wealth my goals,
  just wanting them in the prime of my life, before I get too old.

This Woman of God

This woman of God has many demands,
but she is not a diva.
She is divine and believes in doing the right thing.

This woman of God is flirtatious,
But she advocates fidelity.
She may smile at your man,
But she will always respect man (and his wife).

This woman of God may not go to church,
But she is a Christian
Who believes that one comes to the Father
Through Jesus and his teachings,
Not through an external building.

This woman of God loves to go dancing
But not for the Devil.
Because through God's gift of dance
Neither mind, body, nor spirit is taken for granted.

This woman of God knows she will be judged by others
Based on her acts and beliefs.
But more importantly, this woman of God
Knows that in the end, only God's judgment matters.

Tangela Yvette Cooke

I Think Therefore I Write

The brain is as strong as its weakest think.
-Eleanor Doan

Tangela Yvette Cooke

It's a...Poem!

Artistic conception
in the heart
Intellectual formation
in the mind
Deliverance,
pushed by a pen
Birth on paper
coached by
the rhythm of life
Congratulations,
literary immortality

Tangela Yvette Cooke

Prayer Changes Things

I bow to God, in heaven above.
I say a prayer for the ones I love.

I say a prayer for the teachers in school,
for the brains they fix, education the tool.

I say a prayer for the physicians in white
for healing the sick morning, noon and night.

I say a prayer for the ministers in church,
seeking to save souls, what an endless search.

I say a prayer for the poor and the needy,
poverty the war, helping hands, the treaty.

I say a prayer for the rest of the world:
men, women, children, any and all kind,
to get together and strengthen the bind.

I bow to God in faith and hope
and pray one day we'll be able to cope.

It's About Time

The only thing worse than wasting time
is killing time.
Time is a prerequisite and requisite
for everything we do.
It takes time to make money,
rise to a position of power,
and earn respect.

Time is life's only constant.
It precedes birth and succeeds death –
with you and without you.
Time is what links the past, present and future.
History, evolution and creation
happened over time.

Life's most precious asset is time.
Although it is hard to find free time,
you can spend time…
but you can't save time.
So invest in your time wisely.

Because although time was and always will be…
You may be seconds, minutes, hours, days…
away from losing it.

Tangela Yvette Cooke

Steppin' Into Life

Graduated and now on my own
The world I meet is very unknown-
I must try to reach the goal I promised.
I want to make my family proud and astonished.
It's hard, I know, to start anew,
But other people graduated and made it too.
There is a price I have to pay-
That is to strive and work each day.
There's a purpose for my life that I must fulfill.
It will take introspection, determination and will.
I have a big future but limited time,
And the step I make will be the beginning of mine.

Soul is…

Soul is a combination of hearing and feeling
musical sound waves, vibes or rhythmic sensations
that stimulates your spirit and allows your body
to move poetically synchronized to and with the beat.

Soul is a potpourri, soup or salad of onions,
green peppers, garlic, spices and other
seasonings that gives an accent
and exclamation point to food that wakes up,
tantalizes – then tames your taste buds so fervidly
that while your teeth are doing the cha cha cha
your tongue and cheeks are doing the tango.

Soul is praying to the Lord day in and day out
whether you lose your job, can't feed your
children or can't afford bus fare
and shoes for your feet, but still believing that
God is good all the time.

Soul is emotional, cultural, and spiritual.
Soul, just is.

Tangela Yvette Cooke

Dark and Lovely

"Beauty is in the eyes of the beholder,"
looking down from head to shoulder.

Black is said complexion of one's skin,
many shades of the outside, a soulful feeling within.

Dark is just one description of the word black-
bold and sophisticated, quite stylish in fact.

I proudly state and these eyes can see
that beauty is Dark and Lovely.

Heel to Toe

    The Feet
From this day forward
I want you to know
That I vow to love you
from heel to toe.
    Through Pain
Corns atop
or calluses below
I promise to honor you
from heel to toe.
    In Discomfort
Whether hammer toes above
or heel spurs below
I pledge to support you
from heel to toe.
    or Stress Fractures
Bunions on the side
and arches low
I'll always love you
from heel to toe.

Tangela Yvette Cooke

Diamante Poems

Life
Brief, enduring
Awakening, living, fulfilling
Dreams, birth, burial, funeral
Saddening, frightening, ending
Mournful, grim
Death

Man
Strong, deceitful
Creating, beguiling, protecting
Mechanic, daddy, maid, mother
Nurturing, changing, beautifying
Sensitive, smart
Woman

Depressants
Harmful, addictive
Exhausting, intoxicating, inducing
Alcohol, sleeping pills, caffeine, nicotine
Wakening, exciting, arousing
Cancerous, poisonous
Stimulants

Tangible Times

Stoetry
Poetic storytelling at its best

To know is nothing at all, to imagine is everything.
- Anatole France

Tangela Yvette Cooke

Lucky

"Ding-dong, din-dong," I rung and rung.
No one answered, they must have gone.

Stopped, looked back, and in the air
a cloud of smoke and fire there.

Walking back, back to the house,
screamed little voices all in arouse.

"Help!" cried the voices, that were silent at first.
"Get us out, it's getting worse."

Then through the window and without slack,
I tried to get them children back.

All of their ages – eight, five and one,
lives were saved, before they begun.

I saved them children from smoke and fire,
which started, I learned, from a faulty wire.

Saved them kids with an instinctive glance
and now they've got a second chance.

Tangela Yvette Cooke

A Lesson for Prolific Mamas

for H. Denise Williams

Women, please don't leave your kids inside an empty home alone.
Who knows what might happen or what might go wrong.

Let me tell you a story of a mother that did,
leave a big helpless house with six helpless kids.

She walked down the street to visit her friend,
who watched soaps, gossiped and talked about men.

She too had babies left and right
because of her many sleepless nights.

Now back to that mother:

And so the story began like this.
Keisha Jones had to complete her list.

She walked to the laundry and took a bus to the store.
She had a hair appointment and a meeting at four.

With so many tasks to fulfill alone,
she left her poor kids abandoned at home.

They were there, with nothing to do,
but found some matches and lighted a few.

Fire caught the curtains and the carpeted floor.
It spread to the furniture and the living room door.

as it scattered around, its flames proved fatal.
It killed the five children and the one in the cradle.

Well that's the story and it sure is sad.
Mamas tend to your children, I know Keisha Jones wish she had.

A View to a Kill

On the box last night,
a man killed a girl
for the love of money
and to please the world.
He was acting out his TV role
portraying a sociopath with no soul.

A viewer saw the movie
and was thrilled at this sight,
so mimicked the actor
that was on a death plight.
Influenced by the story's script,
he adopted the role and begin *his* trip.

He raped unsuspecting women
of a certain kind.
The movie had desensitized him,
affected his mind.

Indoctrinated in only 90 minutes
from a television show,
a man learned to murder cleverly
with all systems go.

Oblivious to the creator-
the relationship between TV and life,
Subliminally,
though unintentionally,
suggesting a plot, rope and knife.

Lots of time and energy
expended to ultimately run a reel,
perpetuating continued chaos in life
and the view to a kill.

Tangela Yvette Cooke

Fallen Angel

Extra! Extra! Read the news?
A teenage girl is singing the blues.
High school angel, L7, the best,
flunked an exam, a pregnancy test.

Peers said she was tired of the quiet ways
and had been skipping school for days.
Now whom does she have to blame?
Grades declined. Unexcused absences.
Nobody, it's a shame.

Daddy's sweetheart, his little girl,
he kept her so imprisoned.
he sure messed up. She sure did too,
result, her stomach has risen.

Poor girl, she didn't deserve it,
especially at her age.
But she knew the words no, stop and quit
or to end it at *that* stage.
For a smart girl, her actions were dumb.
Now she'll have to raise a daughter or son.

She refuses to drop out or get and abortion,
she thinks she can raise a kid.
It was her mistake, her decision,
and this child she won't rid.

The father has left, went whoknowswhere
her life, her feelings, he just didn't care.
Responsibilities for the baby are hers
and hers alone.
She has no choice, it was her misfortune
and the father has up and gone.

A baby herself, having to suffer and pay,
learning about life the long, hard way.
A 1 A student, cream of the crop,
has learned a valuable lesson:
If she wants to be wild or just change her ways,
to do it with protection.

Other girls are changing ways also
and making their life a tangle.
They too may end up like her
and become a Fallen Angel.

Day Dreamin'

I went to a concert last night,
and was excited as could be,
yet, while the crowd stamped and hollered
I sat in reverie.

I saw myself standing on stage
dancing and singing my best
then I snapped back, into my skin
to hear "Candy Girl", no less.

New Edition still performed,
but my mind spaced once again.
I was modeling for a captivated audience
and wanted to remain.

Hearing all those voices scream,
I woke up fast, once more,
but gazing at the stage again,
my mind begin to soar.

This time I was on the big screen
acting out a play,
making all my wildest fantasies
happen in a day.

The concert was over, the music ceased,
reality was now my vision,
leaving the arena and going home
was my final and only decision.

In almost two hours, I saw a future
that was only a far-fetched scene,
accepting life as it was before
and realizing sweet dreams.

20/20

With an open mind, I imagined I was blind-
Couldn't see the things around me,
Food, noise, a flower, fall's summer breeze,
I had four senses – I could not see.

The pretty roses, my boyfriend's face,
And everything in every place,
Like rain, the beach, the buzzing bees,
And towering rows of lean palm trees.

Everything was black and as a matter of fact,
The world's shadow on ground,
To picture life, I had to dream
To see the things around.

Then suddenly, I felt within
His beams penetrate my eyes,
I looked up and reconciled
The beautiful blue skies.

I said to God,
You created the light,
And with opened eyes,
I thank You for sight.

Tangela Yvette Cooke

The House that Love Built

To J. Brownlee and D. Russell, for your warmth and hospitality

Down a narrow, winding road
Abruptly ending at a cul-de-sac and guiding one
Up a tangential driveway atop a hill,
Stood a beautiful mansion.
Though this mansion was filled with
Many elegantly furnished rooms and warm fireplaces
Between tall ceilings and marble floors
With staircases strategically designed within an architectural maze,
Its perfectly placed art and memorabilia
That one could visibly inhale
Was most impressive.
Portraits, busts, paintings and black and white pictures
Inspired, no doubt, by love and affection
Coupled with respect, passion and admiration
For the institution of marriage and family
Revealed a story and a brief history of its tenants
And how their mansion was truly just a home
And a house that love built.

The Feet, And Nothing But The Feet, So Help Me God

Because you were neglected by aesthetics,
I hid you in the sand.
But you continued to carry me step by step
as I paved my way on land.

I am sorry that I mistreated you
by shoving you in ill-fitted places.
I kicked you around, then hid my abuse
in shoes that revealed no traces.

You helped me to dance, stomp, run and walk
without massages or accolades.
You've braced me, kept me standing tall
through blister and no first aid.

I apologize for taking you for granted
in my vain and conceited past.
I swear to provide you with care and comfort
to make my only foundation last.

Agony of the feet and bunion surgeries
have opened my heart to you.
I'll learn to love you body and sole
and yes, your pedicure is due.

Tangela Yvette Cooke

You Left

My love, you left, when I needed you more.
You didn't even leave a note on the door.

All of our children...here with me.
Your women...still calling, asking for Lee.

This terrible pain you've left me in,
after all that pleading you would not sin.

Baby, I think you ought to know
that what you've done is very low.

When guilt overwhelms you, you'll finally see
that it was you who left, not the children, nor me.

I-95

Under a teary sky, on turbulent roads,
we ride.
Willfully driven home,
interrupting chats and chuckles,
we scream.
Spontaneously it's struck.
Amongst cries, confusion and fear,
it spins.
Transiently incoherent with life,
the car, a forceful whirlwind,
stops.
The physical and internal anguish,
both ours and the car's,
is silenced.
Abandoning second thoughts, our limbs exit.
We live.
Overjoyed by sirens, relieved by drops,
we speak.
We rejoice.
We pray.

Tangela Yvette Cooke

Tangible Times

Through My Window

We can learn a lot from Mother Nature. She cries. She smiles.
She yells. She has no problem expressing herself.

Tangela Yvette Cooke

The Drought

Thirty dry days in a row
and cumuli out of sight
The morning star's faithful beam
transmits its rays of light

May's abundant green leaves
have turned dry and very brittle
Water bands leave bending blades
begging for just a little

Dolly's threat was just hot air
not a storm or hurricane
Parched petals and thirsty lakes
lament, dying for the rain

Tangela Yvette Cooke

Rain

Reconstituted
Atmosphere
Inspiring
Nature

Sustaining plants, animals and life

Seen during showers
And
Scattered on perfectly sunny days

Too much can drown you
Two little can cause a drought

Touch it, taste it
And take enough
Hold it, it is part of you
And it is wanted and needed as much as
Oxygen

Behold,
look around
It is safe to love it
And it is yours for the taking

Rainbows are beautiful
But rain sustains

Let It Rain

Oh how I long for rain
drizzling down on the grass,
wetting everything in sight;
unpredictable it will pass.

Who else has yearned for rain
(precipitation falling down,
quenching the earth's thirst for life
with the most naturally soothing sound)?

Tangela Yvette Cooke

The Hurricane

The night in dark armor led,
while the wind and rain fought till dead.

The clouds, smoking up the sky,
warned everyone was going to die.

The lightning discharged bolts of shocks,
while the thunder delivered earth moving knocks.

The sun ignited torrid fire
to prove its threats of harm were dire.

Just in time a peaceful front came
to calm the wind and shift the rain.

Though she thought they should have known better,
because the heavens know how to storm the weather.

Rainbows

Beautiful,
Bright,
Brilliant and colorful –
A spectrum of red, orange, yellow, green,
Blue, indigo and violet-
Usually seen
After the rain
When the sun is
Peeking
Through the clouds-
Admire it, remember it, appreciate it,
Because you'll only capture it in a prism.
It is real
But intangible.
You can love it, but it's magic comes and goes.
You can chase it
But you'll never have its pot of gold.
Rainbows never last.

Tangela Yvette Cooke

Tangible Times

Cookie's Corner
1270 N.W. 72nd Street
Miami, Florida 33147

Name   N. E. Adolescent
Address   555 Your Block, Anywhere, Any place 55555

℞

Therapoetic Rhyme & Reason:
poetic expression with out repression for growing pains

Refill <u>2,555</u> Times

<u>*Tangela Y. Cooke*</u>   <u>Lf.d.</u>
                 (signature)

Substitution is allowed unless the prescriber writes 'brand necessary' or 'no substitution'

Tangela Yvette Cooke

Guide to Therapoetic Rhyme & Reason (TRR)

Generic Name
TRR

Brand Names
Poetry
Song
Blues
Rap

Type of Medicine
Antidepressant

Prescribed for
Depression and other growing pains

General Information
The purpose of TRR is to educate, inform or make self and others aware of deep feelings. Unlike other antidepressants, TRR is not taken orally, however, it is taken from the mind and spirit. TRR works by allowing the passage of thoughts, ideas, feelings, and expressions to manifest onto paper. TRR is a mental and spiritual catharsis. Such therapeutic treatment is effective in alleviating common symptoms of depression. It can help improve your mood, wellbeing and life. TRR works the moment it is utilized.

Cautions and Warnings
TRR may not work for everyone. Traditional chemical antidepressants may be recommended. Consult your physician.

Possible Side Effects
Superfluous writing or writer's block that creates sleeplessness. Pity from those more fortunate than you. Criticism and lack of compassion from those who can't relate to you perceived suffering or pain. Judgment by others who are ignorant or who can't understand your struggle. Inspiration.

Drug and Food Interactions
None known

Usual Dosage
Use TRR when consumed or overwhelmed with negative thoughts or if you've become preoccupied with recurring thoughts. In other words, use TRR as needed.

Overdosage
Complete catharsis. Many people have created anthologies, books, journals and music after an overdose of TRR.

Special Information
Continued treatment for the duration of the depression and growing pains is usually required to determine the efficacy of TRR. You may start and stop TRR as much as you like. TRR treatment may lead to positive thoughts, inner peace and inspirational poetry.

Tangela Yvette Cooke

The Essence of Adolescence Part I: I heard you.

You said,
"Dick, will never go out of style,"
to sit back,
relax,
and wait a while.
But
you may as well
divorce me dad
cause I ignored your
advice.
I've made you mad.
Like
curiosity
killed the cat,
experimentation
can
accomplish that,
and the condom
slipped of
yet,
today I live
a solemn promise
to you
I give
to go to school
earn good grades
and success
I know
you expect no less.

You said,
"If you want to see him
or be with him
meet him
on the street."
But I'm no hooker, dad,
and I have a right
to not worship
your ground
and feet.
So,
you may as well
divorce me soon
'cause I love boys,

Tangible Times

my freedom
and my room.
You've silenced yourself,
won't speak to me
'cause you don't like
this boy.
Well
I approve
and you don't know him
and in my heart
there's joy.
Romeo,
Romeo,
wherefore art thou
Romeo.
You say,
"Romeo [Efrain]
is a dog
and I will learn
the hard way.
I say that
I'm sure
father knows best,
but
just not today.
Thus,
today I live
a solemn promise
to you I give
to go to school
earn good grades
and success
I know
you expect no less.

I know
you expect no less.

I know
you expect no less.

Tangela Yvette Cooke

The Essence of Adolescence Part II: Are you listening?

Daddy
I have ideas
and
I love to write
but
my talents
to you
are out of mind,
out of sight.
I gather
I know
it's too great a task
to show
some interest
or break down
and ask.
Sometimes
I'm angry
and feel
rebellious,
but I'm definitely
not wild,
I'm filled with
passion
and adventure
no doubt,
my father's child.
Because
today I live
a solemn promise
to you
I give
to go to school,
earn good grades
and success
I know
you expect no less.

Dad please
release me
from the angelic
image
you have of me.
I'm not perfect

Tangible Times

like
you're not perfect,
so please
let me be.
I'm my own
person
with my own perceptions
and my own
identity.
I have my own
issues,
my own
problems
with individuality.
So
today I live
a solemn promise
to you
I give
to go to school,
earn good grades
and success
I know
you expect no less.

Yes,
I need you
in my life,
but not
to be my friend,
or
to be like your wife.
I need your
love,
support,
encouragement
and your
wisdom from the past.
I need your
ears,
shoulders,
arms,
and your
hugs to make them last.
Through
my rite

Tangela Yvette Cooke

of passage,
I ask for a
divorce
from the memories
of "Daddy's Little Baby."
Please accept me
as the teen
I am
or in essence
a young lady,
and
today I live
a solemn promise
to you
I give
to go to school,
earn good grades
and success,
I know
you expect no less.

I know
you expect no less.

I know
you expect no less.

I Surrender

There is a saying that "Life is a bowl of cherries,"
but now experiencing it, it ain't all that merry.
What is life if it has had no beginning or end?
It has wounds that even God can't mend.
Who says life is worth living,
with so much taking and so little giving?
Who wants to live this life full of sin, illness, hate and crime?
The whole thing, I think, is just a waste of time.
Who appreciates fortune and fame
when this miserable life brings nothing but shame?
Who has time for this nerve-wracking event?
If life were money, it wouldn't be lent.
Who has time to set goals for the future,
in a life going nowhere, a life once started, but not yet there-
a life full of confusion, dishonesty, and mistakes,
a life that's asleep and hardly ever awake?
Lord!
Listen to a child in despair,
a child that doesn't want to live, yet doesn't want to die,
who wants to surrender, and only You know why,
a child who's just existing and wants heaven now.
Suicide? Homicide? Accident? How?
It is peace that I request from you, hoping that I'm heard.
So Father please listen, it's my only word.

Tangela Yvette Cooke

Who Am I?

Who am I to dream the boldest dreams,
that I really want to come true?

Who am I to wake up every morning
to begin a day anew?

Who am I to wonder every night
will I see tomorrow?

Who am I to grieve those hungry souls
that feel my heart with sorrow?

Who am I to shed wells of tears
that bring forth no solution?

Who am I to slander television
that fills minds with pollution?

Who am I to say that I'm not afraid
to walk the streets at night?

Who am I to view my life
as an extremely unfruitful plight?

Who am I to learn the past,
that somehow ain't always proven?

Who am I to question God
about how his world is movin'?

>I will tell you who I think I am.
>I am a girl who's afraid of life,

>Scared silly of living today
>because tomorrow may bring more strife.

>I am intimidated by death, everyone's fright,
>for I think I might miss out.

>I am afraid of what my future will bring
>and what *it's* all about.

>I dread divorce, illness
>and stressful emotional roller coaster rides.

Tangible Times

        I fear greater depression, contracting diseases
        and the contemplation of suicide.

Who am I? That's a good question
for girl who can't decide.

Who lives and then will die,
in the meantime she's torn inside.

Happiness, A Camouflage

No one is aware
of what's behind her facial expression,
especially when she's laughing.

Is she as happy as the world perceives
or does her smile conceal her sorrow?
When things fail to go her way
she grins and thinks, tomorrow.

Her cynical attitude towards serious matters
has made life, to her, a joke.
She's inconsiderate of the feelings of others
and who she might provoke.

She's facetious, elated and frolicsome
just to hide a tear.
She deludes people of her dejected emotions
showing them her cheer.

As luminous as Ms. Monroe,
she'd rate amongst the stars.
She'd probably win a Golden Globe
the way she hides her scars.

She's afraid to reveal both sides of her
she wants not to regret it.
She makes unhappy, doleful times
seem not so pathetic.

In any case, no one knows
of the looks that show her feelings.
Her disguise and false appearance
has no true revealing.

So, what the world sees in their eyes
is only a mirage.
But to her it's a perfected image
and a reliable camouflage.

Think Before You Speak

Who said, "Sticks and stones may break your bones,
but words will never hurt you?"
From observation of such behavior
I know in fact, *words* do…

One experience with speaking my mind
happened while I was a teen.
I was filled with frustration and bound by depression,
a very dreary scene.

With anger locked up inside of me,
just waiting to come out,
I told a man what I thought of him
and told him with no doubt.

While voicing my opinions,
my anger turned to hate.
I confronted him about all of his lies
and did not hesitate.

I spoke out freely
and didn't bite my tongue-
No thoughts or cares about his feelings
or the damage being done.

He responded with silence,
while his expression revealed his hurt.
My bitter heart and loose tongue
just made me feel like dirt.

From my story, you can imagine
how words do hurt at first.
They may not cause physical pain,
but emotionally they're the worst.

Mean words on paper, via phone
and especially face to face,
can make you happy, sad, or angry
in almost any case.

So before you speak of anything,
think of what to say;
and just before your open your mouth,
think about how, the way.

A Tear For a Purpose

I cry sometimes.

In moments of happiness,
I am so proud of myself that I get teary and gay,
and I think that life is really okay.

I cry sometimes.

Because with life comes sorrow,
there are deaths, bad mishaps,
like there's no tomorrow.

I cry sometimes.

In anguish and pain,
from sadness, you know, depression of the mind,
I think suicide is the only way out, because life is unkind.

I cry sometimes.

When I'm angry and can't have my way,
I think someone has betrayed me,
and for my hurt he should pay.

I cry sometimes.

When my disappointments are great,
like failing a test, feeling neglected
or being jilted by a date.

I cry sometimes.

From plain old emotion,
boyfriend problems,
and other devotions.

I cry sometimes.

For accomplishments I've made,
like increasing my knowledge
and making the grade.

I cry sometimes.

For no reason at all,
to rid my bad feelings,
a grievance call.

I cry sometimes.

It's part of me,
and the tears I shed
will always be.

Tangela Yvette Cooke

To Die For

Playing childish pranks,
silly to the core,
a new performance everyday,
this child you can't ignore.

       She was dying for attention.

Excelling in her classes,
trophies on display,
scholastics a priority,
she was trying to make a way.

       She was dying for recognition.

Longing to be kissed,
yearning for his touch,
with warm inviting skin,
she wanted him so much.

       She was dying for affection.

Praying everyday,
repenting for her sins,
conceding He was Lord,
she hoped to make amends.

       She was dying for forgiveness.

Feeling like an alien,
yet wanting to fit in,
not worthy to be their daughter in law,
she was too different to be their friend.

       She was dying for acceptance.

Weakening to a lub,
spiritually declining,
brain cells fading one by one,
giving up, this girl is dying.

       Giving up, this girl is dying.
Dying
Dying
Dying

Sticks and Stones

Skinny,
Awky,
Retard...

Sticks and stones
may break your bones,
but words
can crush your self-image,
self-esteem, and self-confidence,
causing serious harm.

Who are you kidding?
Words can hurt you,
just like sticks and stones.

Sometimes
having a sense of humor
won't protect you
from ridicule, belittlement and taunt,
just like your fists can't defend you
from sticks and stones.

Such verbal abuse
can penetrate
your [emotional] armor,
just like sticks and stones.

Calling a child
"Skinny"
"Bony"
"Bald-headed"
"Awky"
"Retard"
"Weird"
"Crazy"
etc.
can tear and wound
her [emotional] flesh,
just like sticks and stones.

Just words, you say.
I can still hear them today.
How injurious.
How damaging.
How hurtful.
Just like sticks and stones.

Tangela Yvette Cooke

Metamorphic

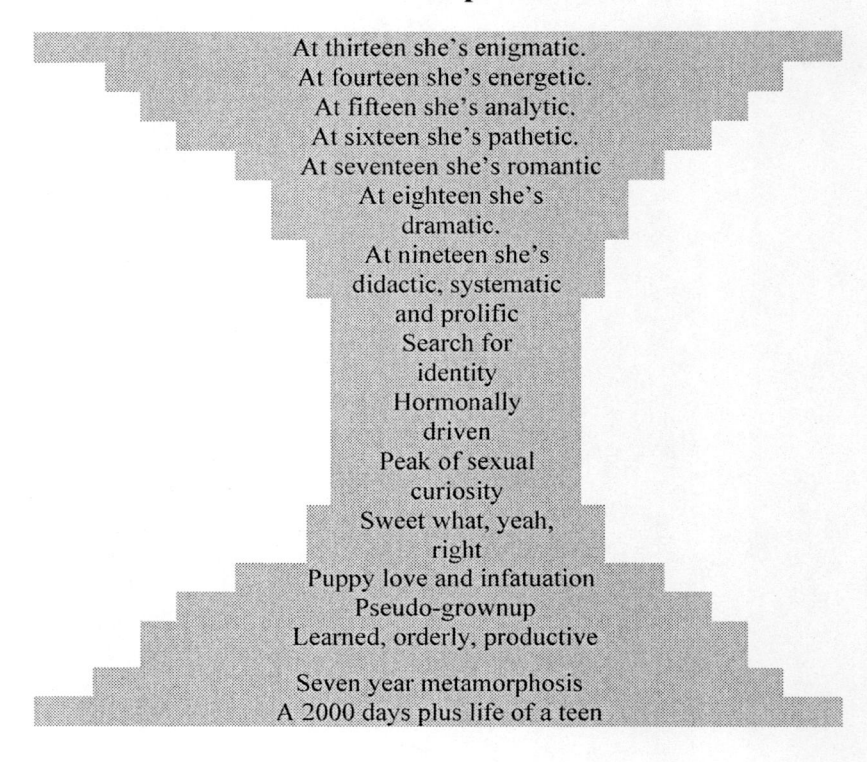

At thirteen she's enigmatic.
At fourteen she's energetic.
At fifteen she's analytic.
At sixteen she's pathetic.
At seventeen she's romantic
At eighteen she's
dramatic.
At nineteen she's
didactic, systematic
and prolific
Search for
identity
Hormonally
driven
Peak of sexual
curiosity
Sweet what, yeah,
right
Puppy love and infatuation
Pseudo-grownup
Learned, orderly, productive

Seven year metamorphosis
A 2000 days plus life of a teen

Debutante

Conception, an embryo, a fetus,
thus, a child brought to the earth
to face trials and tribulations
proceeding her birth.

Like a foreigner, she enters a place
that's truly unknown to her,
interpreting life from what she sees
and sometimes it's a blur.

Miss Teenager, enduring in clothes,
shopping her greatest adventure,
adults, small jobs, and fortunate findings,
her source of expenditure.

An adolescent, a blossoming bud
reaching the spurts of puberty,
transforming to a beautiful flower,
so that God's world can see.

Almost, but not quite yet,
a woman to desire-
she must be well informed of the birds and the bees,
and all else to acquire.

A girl through the stages,
who is strong, sensitive
and most of all smart
has surpassed all that was shady,
making her debut in life, her public appearance
as a refined, young woman, a lady.

Tangela Yvette Cooke

Permission

Dedicated to Guichard Cadet

You don't have to conceal...
With your issues, just deal.
Rant, if you will...
It's justifiable to feel...
Your emotions are real...
Not emitting makes you ill...
Ironically, emptying can fill...
And imploding can kill...
If it helps, please reveal...
Don't accept...and sit still.
Because through feeling and being we heal.

Discouraged

She wants to exploit and challenge her intellect.

He questions her objectives.

She wants to animate and disclose her mind.

He says her imagination is not universal.

She wants to vicariously exchange with someone else's lifestyle.

He says stick to acquired wisdom.

She wants to reiterate and paraphrase archaic expressions.

He says be original and develop anew.

She wants to deviate from structure and grammar.

He says consult your local lexicon.

I say give your distorted mind a rest and lay your pencil down.

Tangela Yvette Cooke

To the Kidz,

From Auntie

Do your best, make the wisest decision, and then relax.
- Thomas B. Smith

Tangela Yvette Cooke

Children

Skinny,
Tall,
Dark,
Light,
Children are a beautiful sight.

A students, D students – they're unique to the core.
Encourage them, discipline them, but please don't ignore…!
Sometimes they're rebellious and may make mistakes.
But please don't abandon them, for God's sake!
They're human!
They're young people who deserve respect!
They have needs, especially to feel loved,
so please don't neglect…!
They live what they learn.
They learn what they see.
So don't show them abuse and addiction
and not teach them to be free!

Teacher's pet,
Scholar,
Pain in the butt
Cherish your children no matter what.

Tangela Yvette Cooke

The Brain

The brain is like a battery,
charged and ready to go.

If you use it wisely,
it will go to and fro.

It's also like a battery in a couple of other ways.
It doesn't like to sit for days and days and days.

And if you do not use it and just let it lay about,
it will do what you've allowed it to do – sit there and die out.

Why Homework?

Who knows why they give us homework?
To get revenge? To make us smart?
Do teachers give us homework because they don't have a heart?

Maybe it's for the future,
to teach us along the way, or
maybe it's because they're mean and want to make us pay.

Who knows why they give it to us?
We do enough work in class,
but we have to do it anyway; it's probably to help us pass.

Why Homework?

Is it clear,
why it's part of the pedagogy, or
does it just echo like Hamlet's question?: "To be or not to be…?"

Tangela Yvette Cooke

The Courageous One

He watches over his loved ones
with his eyes and his gun,
always making sure his work is done.

The brave one, they say,
he who protected them night and day,
was killed – for his courage he pays.

The Mind

The throne of consciousness
And all things complex
Thinking and feeling
What will be processed next
Resolutions, plans, functioning right
Headaches
And resting at night
Why me
Because I rule the body

Tangela Yvette Cooke

About the Author

Tangela Yvette Cooke is a native of Florida. She was educated at the University of Miami where she completed a Bachelor's Degree in Communication. She began writing in "Cookie's Corner" at the age of fifteen. She lives and continues to write in Atlanta, Georgia.